Christian Doctrine

A Book of Basic Beliefs

FOREWORD

During the 1991 National Conference of the Churches of Christ in Zimbabwe there was an appeal from the youth of the churches for a study book to be prepared that would contain teachings of the church that the young people should know. For several years before that it had been felt that a good study book was needed, not just for the youth, but for church leaders and potential church leaders as well.

To meet this need, missionaries at Mashoko Mission, particularly David Grubbs, Peter Grubbs, and Jill Shaw pooled their efforts and produced this manuscript. The material was then published by the Central Africa Mission Evangelistic Literature Service (C.A.M.E.L.S.) in Masvingo, Zimbabwe. For a number of years this mission publishing house has been overseen by Frances Johnson. The book came to the attention of the director of The Christian Restoration Association who was much impressed with the quality of both its contents and format. Realizing that it could be a blessing to churches in America, he sought and gained permission to publish it in the States. Only a minimum of editing, most of it to make the book more applicable to an American audience, was done.

An interesting aspect concerning this book is that the authors acknowledge their use of notes from various Bible teachers and specifically refer to the use of unpublished work of the late Professor George Mark Elliott. Professor Elliott was for many years a faithful trustee of the Christian Restoration Association.

It is hoped that the book will be widely used to instruct Christians in the basic doctrines of the church.

Unless otherwise indicated, the New International Version (NIV) has been used.

TABLE OF CONTENTS

Chapter 1 – THE GOD OF THE BIBLE

God has revealed himself to us in different ways. The earth, sun, moon, and stars declare the glory of God (Psalm 19:1). The apostle Paul said that the coming of rain, the harvest of crops, and even the joy found in the heart of man tell us of the kindness of God (Acts 14:17). Paul told the men of Athens that the presence of so many races of people living in their places on earth should cause men to reach out to God (Acts 17:26, 27). God had revealed himself to man before sin entered the world (Romans 1:20), but people chose to forget what they knew about God (Romans 1:25, 28).

The special revelation of God is the Bible and the perfect revelation of God is seen in Jesus Christ. The Old Testament prophets taught people about God, but Jesus is His exact revelation (Hebrews 1:1-3). That is why we who are Christians must base our understanding of God and our knowledge of God on Jesus and His teachings. He said of himself, "Anyone who has seen me has seen the Father' (John 14:9). We know God only as we know Jesus and His church.

When men gave up their knowledge of God (Romans 1:25, 28), they developed new ideas of their own. Some worshiped spirits that lived in trees, in mountains, or in rivers. Others worshiped spirits that lived in animals or were spirits of departed ancestors. Some, like the Greeks, had many gods which they worshiped. Idols were made of wood, stone, or metal and these were thought to have special powers (Jeremiah 10:3-5, 14-16). Some people even said that there is no god at all.

The Bible teaches us many things that God wishes us to know about himself.

GOD HAS ALWAYS EXISTED

He did not create himself. The heathens find a beginning time for their gods. The god of Egypt, Ra, said, "I created myself." He came from nothing so it would have been impossible for him to speak before he existed. When Moses asked God for His name, God said He was the "I AM" (Exodus 3:14). He meant that He is the One who has always existed. Jesus also said of himself, "Before Abraham was, I am" (John 8:58).

The Bible begins with the words, "In the beginning God created the heavens and the earth" (Genesis 1:1). He existed before anything was created. This is also the meaning of John 1:1-3. So God is eternal. Moses said, "From everlasting to everlasting, you are God" (Psalm 90:2). God says of himself, "I am the Alpha and the Omega, . . . who is, and who was, and who is to come, the Almighty" (Revelation 1:8). God, who has always existed, will never come to an end.

GOD IS A PERSON

God has the emotional and reasonable qualities that we expect to find in people rather than in animals. The Bible often speaks of the emotional and ethical nature of God. He is loving and patient (John 3:16; 2 Peter3:9; Romans5:6-8; 1 John 3:1). He is jealous (Exodus 20:4-6; 1 Corinthians 10:22). He is gentle (Isaiah 40:11).

These are only a few of the qualities that teach us that God is a person.

GOD IS HOLY

This means that God is spiritually pure. There is nothing morally or ethically wrong with God. It is impossible for there to be any evil found in God (Isaiah 6:3; 1 Peter 1:15, 16; Leviticus 19:2; Revelation 4:8).

GOD HAS NO LIMITATIONS

All power belongs to God (Psalm 115:3; Isaiah 43:13; Matthew 19:26). There is no weakness in Him, and nothing in the universe has more power.

He has all knowledge (Hebrews 4:13; 1 John 3:20; Proverbs 15:3). His knowledge is so great that the knowledge of men is foolishness with God (1 Corinthians 1:20).

He is always present (Psalm 139:8; Acts 17:27). His Spirit is everywhere. There is no place where He cannot be found. We do not have to search for Him because He is always present among us.

GOD IS FOUND IN THREE PERSONS: THE FATHER, THE SON, AND THE HOLY SPIRIT

This is a very difficult thing to learn. We are not wise enough to understand it, but because the Bible teaches that it is so, we must accept this truth. There are no illustrations in human experience which can give us a good example of this teaching. We will see what the Bible says.

There are religious groups who stumble over this truth and who reject Christianity because they cannot accept that God is found in three persons. They are the Jewish faith, Islam, the Jehovah's Witnesses (Watchtowers), the Mormons (Latter Day Saints), as well as others.

In Genesis chapter 1, we find the account of the creation of the universe and in it we find God saying, "Let us..." (Genesis 1:26). The Bible tells us that Jesus was present with God and "through him all things were made; without him nothing was made that has been made" (John 1:2, 3). Paul said, "By him all things were created: things in heaven and on earth, visible and invisible, whether thrones or powers or rulers or authorities; all things were created by him and for him. He is before all things, and in him all things hold together" (Colossians 1:16, 17). Paul also tells us that Jesus was on an equality with God (Philippians 2:6). We are instructed to baptize in the name (not names) of the Father, and the Son, and the Holy Spirit (Matthew 28:19). We will learn more about this in the next three chapters.

SUMMARY

The God of the Bible has revealed himself to us by a special revelation, the Bible. He is a person who is eternal, holy, and without limitations. He is one but is found in three persons: the Father, the Son, and the Holy Spirit. He does not tolerate any other gods and requires all of His creation to be in subjection to Him and to worship Him. His purpose for His creation is to save people from sin so they can enjoy His presence for eternity.

ADDITIONAL STUDY

1. Consider the following Scripture references dealing with the sovereignty of God: Deuteronomy 4:39; 1 Chronicles 29:12; Job 9:12; Psalm 29:10; 47:2; 83:18; 93:1; 135:6; Daniel 2:20; 4:35; Matthew 6:13; Acts 17:24; Romans 9:19.

2. What does the Bible mean when it says that God is holy (1 Peter 1:15, 16)?

3. In John 1:1, who is the Word? Explain verses 2, 14, and 18.

4. We say that we can only know God when we know Jesus. Explain by using Colossians 2:9 and other verses to support this truth.

Chapter 2 – GOD, THE FATHER

When Jesus referred to God, He most commonly addressed Him as "Father." He also encouraged His followers to consider God as their Father. This is not true of non-Biblical religions. If we did not have the Bible, we might think of God as creator, or judge, or provider, but we would not call Him "Father." The concept of the fatherhood of God is one we have been taught from the Bible.

The Old Testament sometimes refers to God as Father, but it is usually in reference to the special relationship God had with the nation of Israel, where they are pictured as His children (Hosea 11:1; Isaiah 1:2; Deuteronomy 1:31; 8:5). During the life of Jesus, the Jews preferred to call themselves the "sons of Abraham," rather than the "children of God" (John 8:33, 53).

THE SPECIAL RELATIONSHIP OF THE FATHER
WITH JESUS

The relationship of God, the Father, and Jesus, the Son, is different from the Father-child relationship that we have with God. Jesus acknowledged the superiority of the Father saying, 'The Father is greater than I" (John 14:28). It was the Father who sent Him (John 15:21; 16:5), and who taught Him (John 8:28). The

Father committed all things to Jesus by placing them in His hands (Matthew 11:27; John 3:35). He gave Jesus the words to speak (John 17:8) and sent angels to minister to Him (Matthew 4:11; Luke 22:43). The Father acknowledged Jesus as His Son at Jesus' baptism (Matthew 3:17) and at His transfiguration (Matthew 17:5). Jesus acknowledged God as His Father in His prayers (John 17:1), in His preaching (John 5:43), and in His parables (Matthew 21:37). The relationship between the Father and the Son was such that Jesus said, "He who hates me hates my Father as well" (John 15:23).

Although there was a superiority of the Father over the Son (John 14:28), there was also an equality that was recognized by those who heard Jesus preach (John 5:18). It was not an equality that Jesus demanded, but one that He obediently accepted (John 15:10; Philippians 2:6; Hebrews 5:8).

GOD IS THE FATHER OF BELIEVERS

Jesus taught that believers should recognize God as their Father and submit themselves to Him as obedient children. When the disciples asked Jesus to teach them to pray, He said, "This, then, is how you should pray: Our Father in heaven..." (Matthew 6:9). We recognize God is our Father when we are morally and ethically His children. It is a relationship for those who believe and do His will (Psalm 103:13; Matthew 5:44, 45). Paul says that we were not His children when we were slaves to sin. God adopted us as His children and has given us the spirit of sonship (Romans 8:12-16). Jesus taught this same lesson (John 8:34, 35). Our sonship is a gift given to us when we are adopted into the family of God. Then we can call Him Father.

GOD IS NOT THE FATHER OF UNBELIEVERS

We are not taught in Scripture that God is the Father of all people. He is their creator. It is physically possible to be the father of a child but, because of conflicting circumstances, not to have a father-child relationship. Paul referred to people who were not ethically and morally God's children as "slaves to sin" (Romans 6:6, 16, 17, 20). He told Elymas, "You are a child of the devil. . . (Acts 13:10). Jesus told the Jews, "You belong to your father, the devil, and you want to carry out your father's desire" (John 8:44).

GOD WANTS TO BE THE FATHER OF ALL PEOPLE
The Bible is an account of what God has done to restore His creation to the original relationship it had with Him. Men were created "in the image and the likeness of God" (Genesis 1:26). Every person on earth has the potential to be a child of God. Jesus told the parable of the loving father (Luke 15:11-32). In it we see how God, the Father, is waiting for the slave to sin to return to Him to be the serving son. This work of redemption is made possible by His "only begotten Son, Jesus."

WHO IS A CHILD OF GOD?
This is a question that John answers in 1 John. He says, "This is how we know who the children of God are and who the children of the devil are" (1 John 3:10).

A child of God is:
    a. a person who does what is right (1 John 3:7-10).
    b. a person who loves his brother (1 John 3:10).
    c. a person who acknowledges Jesus as Lord (1 John 2:23; 4:15).
    d. a person who gives to the needy (1 John 3:17).
    e. a person who is willing to lay down his life for his brother (1 John 3:16).
    f. a person who is disciplined by God (Hebrews 12:4-7).
    g. a person who obeys the commands of God (1 John 3:24; Matthew 7:21).

"We know that we are the children of God, and that the whole world is under the control of the evil one. We know also that the Son of God has come and has given us understanding, so that we may know him who is true. And we are in him who is true—even in his Son Jesus Christ. He is the true God and eternal life. Dear children, keep yourselves from idols "(1 John 5:19-21).

SUMMARY

The Bible opens to us the knowledge that God is Father. He is the Father of His Son, Jesus Christ. That is a special relationship that men cannot have with Him. He is not the Father of all men, even though He is their creator and provider. He is the Father of those who believe on Jesus Christ and who keep His commandments. As the Father, He is greater than the Son, but as our Father, we are comforted to know that He cares for us (Matthew 7:7-12).

ADDITIONAL STUDY

1. Teachings about the fatherhood of God by the apostle John: Read the Gospel of John, chapters 14-17. Read 1 John, chapters 3-5. Write down all references to God as Father and the references to His children.

2. Read the following parables of Jesus and discuss what they teach about God the Father:
    *   The Friend at Midnight   Luke 11:5-13
    *   The Wedding Banquet   Matthew 22:1-14
    *   The Two Sons   Matthew 21:28-32
    *   The Lost Sheep   Matthew 18:10-14
    *   The Wicked Tenants   Luke 20:9-18

Chapter 3 – JESUS, THE SON OF GOD

In this chapter we shall see what Jesus had to say about himself. The apostles taught and believed that Jesus was God who had come in the flesh to redeem the world from sin and to teach men more fully what God wanted to find in their lives. Paul calls Him, "God's indescribable gift" (2 Corinthians 9:15). He is called "Lord of both the dead and the living" (Romans 14:9), "the Lord of glory" (1 Corinthians 2:8), "the chief cornerstone" (Ephesians 2:20), "the head of the church" (Ephesians 5:23), "the source of eternal salvation" (Hebrews 5:9), "the Savior of the world" (1 John 4:14). There is no question that the apostles believed on Him as the Son of God and that they ascribed to Him deity (Colossians 2:9), but we shall see what Jesus said about himself.

JESUS CLAIMED TO BE THE SOURCE OF SALVATION

The disciples were to believe in God; they were also to believe in Jesus (John 14:10). It would be better to have a great millstone hanged around one's neck and be cast into the sea rather than to cause one of the little ones who believed in Him to stumble (Mark 9:42). Those who refused to believe in Him would die in their sins (John 8:24). Not to believe in Him was sin (John 16:8, 9).

Jesus felt it proper that people should worship Him. He accepted worship. In Matthew 14:33, after Jesus came to the disciples by walking on the water, they worshiped Him saying, "Truly you are the Son of God." Jesus asked the man born blind, "Do you believe in the Son of Man?" The man replied, "Who is he, sir?.. . 'Tell me so that I may believe in him?" Jesus said to him, "You have now seen him; in fact, he is the one speaking with you." The blind man said, "Lord, I believe, " and worshiped Him (John 9:35-38). There is no instance in which Jesus refused to be worshiped as did Peter (Acts 10:25, 26) or the angel (Revelation 22:8, 9). He encouraged men to reverence Him. He said that holy men and good angels would refuse to accept worship (Matthew 23:8-10).

Jesus did not permit anything or anyone else to be put above Him, but demanded first place in the lives of men. "Follow me" admitted no compromise (Luke 9:57-62; Mark 10:21). "Anyone who loves his father or mother more than me is not worthy of me;... and anyone who does not take his cross and follow me is not worthy of me" (Matthew 10:37, 38). "In the same way, any of you who does not give up everything he has cannot be my disciple" (Luke 14:33). "One is your Master, even Christ" (Matthew 23:10; KJV).

So here is a young man, just past his thirtieth birthday who demands that all men everywhere submit to Him without reservation, and if they do not, they will be unworthy of Him and will not find salvation.

JESUS CLAIMED THAT ONLY BY HIS DEATH AND RESURRECTION WOULD SALVATION COME TO THE WORLD

Jesus did not just point the way to God, but said He was the way itself (John 14:6). He was not the first Christian; He is the center of Christianity. No one could come to the Father except by Him (John 14:6). Those who confessed Him would be saved, and those who denied Him would be lost (Matthew 10:32, 33; John 12:48; Mark 8:35-38; John 8:24).

His work was to do that which no other man could do. He must die and be resurrected from the dead (John 2:19-22; John 3:14; Mark 8:31; 9:31; Matthew 16:21; Luke 9:22). "The Son of Man (came) . . . to give His life as a ransom for many" (Matthew 20:28). "This is my blood of the new testament, which is shed for many for the remission of sins" (Matthew 26:28; KJV). "I lay down My life, that I might take it again. No man taketh it from me, but I lay it down of myself. I have power to lay it down, and I have power to take it again" (John 10:17, 18; KJV).

The Lamb of God must die for the sins of the world. "O fools, and slow of heart to believe all that the prophets have spoken: Ought not Christ to have suffered these things, and to enter into his glory? And beginning at Moses and all the prophets, he expounded unto them in all the scriptures the things concerning himself" (Luke 24:25-27; KJV). "This is what is written: The Christ will suffer and rise from the dead on the third day, and repentance and forgiveness of sins will be preached in his name to all nations, beginning at Jerusalem" (Luke 24:46, 47).

JESUS CLAIMED THAT HE HAD THE AUTHORITY TO FORGIVE SINS

Many of us can tell people how sins may be forgiven, but Jesus claimed the authority to forgive sins. "Son, your sins are forgiven" (Mark 2:5). He connected forgiveness of sins with His own person. The scribes charged Him with blasphemy and said, "Who can forgive sins but God only?" (Mark 2:7). To refute the charge of blasphemy, He said, "The Son of Man has authority on earth to forgive sins" (Mark 2:10.) He then demonstrated His power with a miracle of healing.

JESUS CLAIMED THAT HE HAS ALL AUTHORITY
IN HEAVEN AND ON EARTH

He included himself with the Father and the Holy Spirit at baptism in such a way as to claim an equal deity and authority (Matthew 28:18-20). "In the world ye shall have tribulation: but be of good cheer; I have overcome the world" (John 16:33; KJV). "I am going there to prepare a place for you. ... I will come back and take you to be with me that you also may be where I am" (John 14:2, 3).

SUMMARY

Jesus cannot be ignored. He is by far the most important person to have walked the face of the earth. He claimed to be God who came down from Heaven to live as a man and to die and be resurrected, so that those who believe on Him might have eternal life. He claimed that there was no other way to find salvation other than through Him. Some said He was mad (Mark 3:21), and others said He had a demon (John 10:20) or was Satan himself (Mark 3:22). It He is who He claimed to be, then He is "Christ our Savior" (Titus 1:4) and Jesus, the Son of God.

ADDITIONAL STUDY

1. Jesus is called the "Cornerstone." What did He mean in Matthew 21:44 when He said, "He who falls on this stone will be broken to pieces, but he on whom it falls will be crushed"?

2. Why did Jesus also identify himself as the Son of Man? (John 3:13; Matthew 9:6; John 6:53; Luke 21:27; John 5:27).

3. Read Hebrews 9:11-28 and answer the question: "Why could God not forgive sins by any other way except by the death and resurrection of Jesus?"

Chapter 4 – THE HOLY SPIRIT

The amount of both Old Testament and New Testament Scriptures that teaches about the Holy Spirit is amazing. It is far too much to consider in one lesson. However, we will examine a few references to help us begin to know and to understand the Holy Spirit and His work.

The Old Testament teaches that the Holy Spirit assisted in the creation of the world (Genesis 1:1, 2, 26). He also gave God's servants power, wisdom, and courage so that they could do their God-given work (Judges 6:34; 11:29; 14:6; Exodus 31:3; Numbers 11;17, 25; 1 Samuel 16:13, 14; Nehemiah 9.20). The writing of the Old Testament itself is a work of the Holy Spirit and demonstrates why it is completed by the New Testament, the two being one book (2 Samuel 23:2; Zechariah 7:12; 2 Timothy 3:16; 2 Peter 1:21). The Holy Spirit in the Old Testament helped to prepare for the coming of Jesus and to make His person and work to be seen as part of God's plan for the salvation of men.

THE HOLY SPIRIT IS A DIVINE PERSON

The Holy Spirit has a mind which knows the will of God and searches the deep things in God. He also knows the mind of men

(Romans 8:27; 1 Corinthians 2:10, 11). He has love (Romans 15:30). He has emotions and qualities which can be offended. We can blaspheme Him (Matthew 12:31, 32), lie to Him (Acts 5:3), resist Him (Acts 7:51), grieve Him (Ephesians 4:30), insult Him (Hebrews 10:29), and put out His fire within us (1 Thessalonians 5:19).

THE HOLY SPIRIT WAS PROMISED TO THE APOSTLES

Jesus assured the apostles during His ministry that they would be helped by the coming of the Holy Spirit (Matthew 10:17-20; Mark 13:11; John 16:12-15; Luke 24:45-49; Acts 1:4, 8). The fulfillment of these promises is seen in the book of Acts and in the writing of the other New Testament books. They were told that He would "convict the world of guilt in regard to sin, and righteousness, and judgment" (John 16:8-11). This was fulfilled in the ministry of the apostles. The Holy Spirit gave them a message (Acts 2:4) which caused men to be convicted and to turn to Jesus in repentance and baptism (Acts 2:36-41). The apostles were baptized with the Holy Spirit (Acts 2:1-4) who gave them miraculous powers (Acts 3:2-10) which they could give to others by the laying on of their hands (Acts 6:6; 8:5-8, 17-19; 19:6). There is no evidence in the Bible that this gift of giving the Holy Spirit by the laying on of hands was passed on to others by the apostles. In other cases of laying on of hands, it was for the purpose of setting people apart for some special work (Acts 13:3; 1 Timothy 5:22). It was the Holy Spirit who led the apostles and the early church in their preaching (Acts 8:39; 11:12; 13:4; 16:6, 7).

THE HOLY SPIRIT WAS PROMISED TO BAPTIZED BELIEVERS

Those who obey the gospel in repentance and baptism are promised the gift of the Holy Spirit (Acts 2:38; 5:32). This is sometimes called the ordinary gift because it is not associated with miraculous powers. It is promised to every immersed believer. The indwelling presence of the Holy Spirit in the lives of Christians testifies to them (Romans 8:16) and helps them pray (Romans 8:26). Christians are sealed with the Spirit (Ephesians 1:13, 14). He sanctifies them (Romans 15:16; 1 Corinthians 6:11), helps them in their infirmities (Romans 8:26), makes intercession for them (Romans 8:26), and guides them (Romans 8:14). The body is the temple of the Holy Spirit (1 Corinthians 6:19, 20).

Out of the life of the Christian comes fruit as found in Galatians 5:22-25 and in 2 Timothy 1:7. At the last the Holy Spirit will raise Christians from the grave (Romans 8:11).

Paul said, "There is. . . one baptism" (Ephesians 4:4, 5), and it is always associated with the gift of the Holy Spirit (Acts 2:38). It is the baptism of the Great Commission and it will be in force until the end of the world (Matthew 28:18-20).

THE BAPTISM (OUTPOURING) OF THE HOLY SPIRIT

There are two recorded special outpourings of the Holy Spirit in the New Testament. The apostles were baptized in the Holy Spirit on the Day of Pentecost (Acts 2:1-4). This was accompanied by a mighty sound which filled the house and with tongues like flames which sat on the apostles. Following this, they were able to speak in other languages, as the Spirit gave them the message, and to do miraculous works.

The second recorded baptism of the Holy Spirit was on Cornelius and his household (Acts 10:44). It was used to convince the Jews that the gospel was now to be preached to the Gentiles (Acts 10:47; 11:1-18). It did not bring them pardon for their sins (Acts 15:9; 11:18; 10:47, 48), nor did it take the place of water baptism (Acts 10:47, 48). It was related to the baptism of the apostles on Pentecost (Acts 11:15).

SUMMARY

There is . . . one Spirit (Ephesians 4:4). He is often found together with the Father and the Son: in creation (Genesis 1:1, 2, 26), at the baptism of Jesus (Matthew 3:16, 17), in the teaching of Jesus (John 14:16), and in the Great Commission (Matthew 28:19). The three are also found together in Heaven (Revelation 14:1, 13). He is the Spirit of Truth (John 14:17). He does not lie nor work contrary to the Scriptures which He gave through inspiration. The one Spirit leads to the one way of salvation through Jesus Christ. He came to glorify Jesus and to lead the lost to find Him.

ADDITIONAL STUDY

Passages which may help in study are Psalm 51:10-12; Psalm 143:10; Isaiah 63:8-14; Joel 2:28-32; John 16:5-15; Galatians 5:16-26; Revelation 22:17-20.

Chapter 5 – SPECIAL GIFTS OF THE HOLY SPIRIT: TONGUES, PROPHECY, AND HEALING

There is much confusion and division in the church because of a difference in understanding of the special gifts of the Holy Spirit. A review of chapter 4, The Holy Spirit, shows that He is the Spirit of Truth (John 14:17). He does nothing contrary to His Word, the Bible, which He gave us through inspiration (2 Timothy 3:16; 2 Peter 1:21). A clear understanding of the Bible will help us put away the confusion and division over the matter of the special gifts.

THE UNITY OF THE CHURCH

Jesus prayed for the unity of the church (John 17:22). Paul was also concerned about things which divided the church (1 Corinthians 1:10). Some of the divisions were caused by people who did not understand the purpose of the Old Testament law (Romans 4:13-25; Galatians 3:25) and wanted to impose Jewish practices on the new Christian (Acts 15:1, 2). Other divisions were caused by ignorance of the purpose and use of the special gifts of the Holy Spirit (1 Corinthians 12-14). We need to know that the unity of the church and Christian love must be preserved and that the Holy Spirit would do nothing to destroy the fellowship of the church.

SPEAKING IN TONGUES

The first recorded event of the speaking in tongues in the New Testament was that of the apostles on the day of Pentecost (Acts 2:1-12). These are called other tongues, or unknown tongues, and in further reading of the passage are found to be languages which had not been previously spoken by the apostles. These languages were understood by people from many places outside Jerusalem (Acts 2:8). They were languages which were unknown by the speaker, but were understood by the hearers.

The next time the event is mentioned is at the home of Cornelius when he and his household spoke in tongues (Acts 10:46). Peter likened the event to what happened to the apostles on the day of Pentecost (Acts 10:47), so we assume that Cornelius and his household also spoke in a language which was not known to the speaker but was understood by the hearer. This event also occurred in Ephesus when Paul laid his hands on twelve men recently baptized (Acts 19:6). In that the writer of the book of Acts made no distinction between the three events, we assume they are identical in nature.

In 1 Corinthians, Paul discusses the spiritual gifts, and he makes several important points concerning speaking in tongues.

1. Those who speak by the Spirit will not speak anything contrary to the teachings of the Bible (1 Corinthians 12:3).
2. The tongues were a language which could be understood and interpreted by other people (1 Corinthians 14:10; 12:30; 14:5, 13, 28).
3. People should not speak publicly in these languages unless there is someone to interpret to the church (1 Corinthians 14:27).

4. The speaking in tongues was temporary and would one day cease (1 Corinthians 13:8).
5. Speaking in tongues was one of the less important gifts. Greater ones were to be desired (1 Corinthians 12:31; 14:1).
6. The mind of the speaker was not improved when he spoke in tongues (1 Corinthians 14:15).
7. The church was not built up by the speaking in tongues as it was with some of the other gifts (1 Corinthians 14:12).

So, in the interest of orderly worship and proper conduct (1 Corinthians 14:40), Paul did not forbid the speaking in tongues (1 Corinthians 14:39), but he discouraged it in public worship. He suggested that it was immature (1 Corinthians 13:11) and that there was a more worthwhile way of public speaking (1 Corinthians 14:19).

It is important to note that speaking in tongues was never given as a test to see who was more spiritual in the church, and that people who use tongues-speaking as such a test do so in violation of the Bible. Paul says, "Tongues.. .are a sign, not for believers but for unbelievers..." (1 Corinthians 14:22). The significance is the activity of the Holy Spirit and not the goodness or power of the person who is speaking.

PROPHECY

In the Bible a prophet is a person who speaks on behalf of a higher spiritual power. We read about prophets of God (1 Samuel 3:20), prophets of Baal and other false gods (1 Kings 18:19) and other false prophets (Mark 13:22). The prophet may speak about the future, but often speaks about the past or the present (1 Samuel 15:10-34; 2 Samuel 12:1-10). What he says may be true or false depending on the source. If it is from the Lord, then it is true. If from a false god, then it is false.

The early church had prophets (Ephesians 4:11; Acts 11:27; 13:1). The church was also troubled by false prophets (2 Peter 2:1; 1 John 4:1; 2 Thessalonians 2:2). It must be remembered that in the early church the New Testament had not yet been written, so people could not study the words of Jesus or of the apostles to determine truth. Certain men and women had the gift of prophecy (Acts 21:8, 9). They were given messages from God for the people of the church.

The apostles were concerned that the church would be able to understand the gift of prophecy. They taught that:

1. The gift of prophecy was one of a number of unifying gifts in the church (Romans 12:4-6; 1 Corinthians 12:10).

2. The gift of prophecy would one day cease (1 Corinthians 13:8).

3. The gift of prophecy was not as great as the gift of love (1 Corinthians 13:2).

4. The gift of prophecy was more to be desired than speaking in tongues (1 Corinthians 14:1, 5, 39).

5. Prophecy was to be used for strengthening, encouraging, and comforting the members of the church (1 Corinthians 14:3).

6. Prophecy must be used in an orderly way because the prophet controls the gift. The gift does not control the prophet (1 Corinthians 14:32, 33).

7. There must be people present who can weigh (evaluate) the words of the prophet (1 Corinthians 14:29). This makes it possible to test the words to see if they are true or false (1 Thessalonians 5:19-21; 1 John 4:1).

The last days will be noted by the rise of many false prophets. There are many false prophets today. We believe the gift of prophecy was a gift of limited time, and that it likely ceased when the New Testament was available for people to read. The teaching of Jesus and the apostles was then available for them to discover truth. The gift was not for treating illnesses, or for solving family problems or financial difficulties. It was used for instructing believers. It is important for the church to regard those who claim to be prophets with great care.

MIRACLES

What is a miracle? Some would say that a miracle is an event which is contrary to the natural course of events in outcome or in time. The word "immediately" is very important when considering miracles. What is a miracle in the sense of its use in the Bible? The Bible gives it a more specific use. It is an act of God which He uses to demonstrate His power to teach people that God is approving of the person or the teaching associated with the miracle.

In the ministry of Jesus, we read of many miracles that He accomplished. Here are some of the things that God wanted men to learn from the miracles of Jesus:

1. Jesus had been given authority which was not from this earth. Matthew 9:4-7; 12:1-14; Mark 1:21-28; Luke 5:21-26; John 6:14

2. Faith in Jesus is rewarded. Matthew 15:21-28; Mark 2:5; 5:34; 10:52; Luke 7:1-10

3. The miracle encouraged faith, even at a later time. Matthew 16:5-12; Mark 5:36; Luke 7:18-23

4. God is moved by compassion for human need. Matthew 14:14; 20:29-34; Mark 1:41; 6:34; Luke 7:13

5. Jesus is God made flesh. Matthew 17:24-27; Luke 7:11-17

Jesus reminds us that His work was to preach (Luke 4:40-44) and at last to die for the sins of the world (John 3:14-17).

The miracles of the apostles are often called "signs" (Acts 2:43), and the apostles were sure to deny that it was from their own power, but from God (Acts 3:12, 13). There were times that the apostles were not able to heal the sick (Philippians 2:25-28; 2 Corinthians 12:7-9; 1 Timothy 5:23). They were permitted by God to use miracles when it suited God's purposes. In Acts 28: 1-10, we find Paul, Luke, and others on the Island of Malta. In verse 8 we find Paul placing his hands on a man and healing him by means of a miracle. In verse 9 it says the rest of the people were "cured." This word can mean that they were given medical treatment. It does not need to mean that all were healed by means of miracles.

In the early church, one of the gifts was the gift of healing (1 Corinthians 12:9). We usually take this to mean healing by a miracle which would mean "instant" healing. But not all sick people were healed by miracles. The elders were also instructed to pray over the sick and to anoint them with oil (James 5:14, 15), but note that it was the "prayer offered in faith" which brought about the healing. God still heals. We are encouraged to pray for the sick. If God did not bring about healing, why would there be any reason to pray for recovery? Let us be careful not to call the healing a miracle if it does not meet the purpose of a Bible miracle.

SUMMARY

There is much difficulty in the church today because of the claims of those who say they are using the special gifts from the Holy Spirit. The Holy Spirit is able to give gifts as He wishes, but as the Spirit of Truth, He will never do anything contrary to what the Bible teaches. He will not bring disunity to the church. The Bible says the gifts are temporary, but it does not give a time when the gifts were to be removed. The Christians in Corinth were not yet mature in the faith, and their use of the gifts caused confusion and division in the church. For this reason, Paul told them to limit the use of the gifts and discouraged them from using them in public worship. Great caution must be exercised today. The church must carefully study the matter of the special gifts and see that mature Christian activity will be led by love. The greatest gift is love (1 Corinthians 13:13). Desire the greatest gift!

ADDITIONAL STUDY

1. See how Paul makes a difference between mature and immature behavior in 1 Corinthians 13.

2. Try to find all of the miracles done by Jesus and the apostles to see if you can identify the purpose for which each miracle was done.

Chapter 6 – THE BIBLE, GOD'S WORD

There is a simple children's song that has these words:

> The B-l-B-L-E,
> Yes, that's the Book for me;
> I stand alone on the Word of God,
> The B-l-B-L-E.

Although this is a child's song, it contains two great truths. First, the Bible is the Word of God, and second, the Bible is the book for Christians.

The Word "Bible" means simply "book." It is God's book, written for us. It tells us everything that God wants us to know, from the beginning of the world at creation, to God's plan for us to spend eternity with Him.

The Bible has several names for itself. It calls itself "the word of God" (Hebrews 4:12, 1 Thessalonians 2:13). It says that it contains "living words" passed on to us (Acts 7:38). It also calls itself the Holy Scriptures (Romans 1:2; 2 Timothy 3:15). The word "scripture" means "writing." This is the word used by Jesus and His apostles to describe the Old Testament writings (Matthew 21:42; Romans 15:4).

The Bible contains 66 different books: 39 in the Old Testament and 27 in the New Testament. These were written by many different men over a period of about 1500 years. Moses wrote the first five books in the Old Testament about 1400 years before Christ was born (1400 B.C.) The books of the New Testament were written within a period of about 70 years after the death and resurrection of Christ.

Even though many different men wrote down the words in the Bible, the words themselves came from God. We find many places in the Bible which state that the words written there are from God. We have seen that Moses wrote the first five books of the Bible, called the books of the Law. The laws and commands were actually written by God on tablets of stone and given to Moses (Exodus 24:12). God also spoke through men such as King David (2 Samuel 23:2), and through prophets such as Jeremiah (Jeremiah 1:9).

The authors of the New Testament books also state that their writings are from God. In fact, if we examine 2 Peter 1:20, 21 and 2 Timothy 3:16, 17, we find that all Scripture comes from the mind of God, and was written down by men who were inspired to do so by the Holy Spirit. Jesus promised His followers that they would be given the Holy Spirit so that they would be able to recall Jesus' words (John 14:26). So we know that the words of Jesus which are recorded for us are accurate.

There are other ways that we can tell that the words in the Bible are from God and are true. One way is that the prophecies in the Bible have proved to be accurate. Prophecies written hundreds of years before Jesus was born proved to be true about His birth (Micah 5:2; Luke 2:1-7), about His death (Isaiah 53:9, 12; Luke 23:33), and about His resurrection (Psalm 16:10; Matthew 28:1-6).

Believing that the Bible is the Word of God is important, but it is only the first step. If we believe that the Bible is from God, then we need to study the Word of God and apply it to our lives. Those who are not Christians need to study the Bible because it is in the Bible that we find God's plan for saving us from sin. It is in the Bible that we find that all of us are sinners (Romans 3:23). James 1:21 tells us that we need to receive the Word in order to be saved. Romans 10:17 tells us that faith comes through the Word. So although we know that Jesus Christ is the one who saves us, the Bible is the way that we learn of Jesus Christ and of his saving power.

Those who are Christians also need to study the Word of God. It is through this study of the Word that we grow spiritually (1 Peter 2:2). It is with the knowledge of the Word that we are able to meet the attacks of Satan. Jesus quoted Scripture when He was tempted by Satan in the wilderness (Matthew 4:1-11). In the same way, we are to use the Word to stand up against the devil's schemes (Ephesians 6:11, 17).

Our reading of the Bible should not be casual or without thought (Psalm 1:1, 2). Our reading should be a study, and we need to apply what we learn in our study to our lives. If reading the Bible does not change our lives, or if it does not alter how we live from day to day, then we are deceiving ourselves (James 1:22-25). God has given us the Bible to teach us, train us, and correct us, so that we may be useful, fruitful Christians (2 Timothy 3:16, 17).

We are also warned not to add to or to take away any of the words from the Bible (Revelation 22:18, 19). If we do, we may lose our souls.

HOW ARE WE TO STUDY AND TO USE THE BIBLE?

1. Begin with prayer (John 16:13-15). Pray that the Holy Spirit will open your eyes, hearts, and minds.
2. Read, revise or summarize in your mind what you have read, then read the passage again.
3. Write in a notebook your observations and thoughts.
4. Ask the following questions and write the answers in your notebook.
   - What is the main teaching of this passage?
   - Who are the people in this passage? Who is speaking? About whom is he speaking?
   - What is the key verse of this passage?
   - What does this passage teach me about Jesus?
   - Does this passage point out to me any sin in my life that I must confess and discontinue?
   - Is there any command for me to obey in this passage?
   - Is there any promise for me to receive from this passage?
   - Is there any instruction for me to follow?
5. Memorize Scriptures (Psalm 119:15, 16).
6. Respect what you have read and studied. It is from God.

Chapter 7 – THE CHURCH OF THE BIBLE

The church began in Jerusalem on the day of Pentecost (A. D. 30). With the coming of the Holy Spirit and the preaching of the gospel of salvation for the first time, many accepted the message, believed in Jesus, and were baptized for the remission of their sins. The church began with about three thousand members (Acts 2:37-41). The church is a fellowship of believers, and it was established by Jesus so that His ministry would continue on earth after His ascension into Heaven (Acts 1:8).

There are many pictures used in the New Testament to describe the relationship of the church to Jesus. The church is the bride of Christ (Ephesians 5:22-32; Revelation 21:2) with Jesus the bridegroom (John 3:29). It is a building (1 Corinthians 3:9) with Christ being the builder (Matthew 16:18) and the chief cornerstone (Ephesians 2:19, 20). It is a living body (1 Corinthians 12:18-27; Colossians 1:18; Ephesians 1:22, 23) with Christ as the head of the body (Colossians 2:19). It is a temple (1 Corinthians 3:16; Ephesians 2:21) in which God dwells (Ephesians 2:22).

AUTHORITY IN THE CHURCH

In all of the above pictures of the church, we see that authority belongs to Jesus. He is the Head, the Bridegroom, and the Builder. The pictures show that there are also relationships between the members of the church. They are parts of the body (1 Corinthians 12:12-27) and depend on each other as they are directed by the Head. As parts of a building (Ephesians 2:22; 1 Peter 2:5), Christians must join together to make a temple in which God may dwell. But in all of the pictures the authority does not rest with men but with Christ.

BECOMING A MEMBER OF THE CHURCH

A person does not join the church or take membership in it as one would join an organization of the world. Through the new birth (John 3:3), a person is added to the church (Acts 2:41). All have sinned (Romans 3:23) and have been separated from God's family. Sinners live in a world of evil and are away from God. Because of their sin, they deserve punishment by death (Romans 6:23), but God's great love provided away of escape from death (John 14:6) through His Son, Jesus. Jesus died for us taking away our punishment and our sin (Colossians 2:13, 14).

The Bible teaches that we become a member of the church by dying to our old life (Romans 6:2-6), and by being raised again as a new creature and a child of God (Romans 6:4). This happens in Christian baptism. It requires faith (John 3:36; Acts 16:30, 31), repentance (Luke 15:11-24), confession (Matthew 10:32, 33), and baptism (immersion) in water. Chapter 8 will discuss more about baptism.

THE CHURCH THAT CHRIST BUILT

Through the centuries, ignorance, confusion, and false doctrine have divided the church into many groups. Some of these groups are very far from being the church found in the Bible. In order to please God and to have confidence that we are doing His will, we must try to be as much like the church found in the New Testament as we can possibly be. We must study New Testament commands and examples for the church. Only in this way can we restore the unity and the purity of the church that Christ built (Matthew 16:16).

ADDITIONAL STUDY

If we are trying to restore the church to be the church that Jesus built, what are some of the things that need to be restored?

1. We must restore the names the Bible uses to identify the church and its members.

    a. Names used for the church in the New Testament:

◆ the church of Christ	Romans 16:16
◆ the body of Christ	Ephesians 1:22, 23
◆ the churches of God	1 Corinthians 11:16
◆ the household of God	1 Timothy 3:15
◆ the flock of God	Acts 20:28
◆ the church of the firstborn	Hebrews 12:23
◆ the church of the saints	1 Corinthians 14:33
◆ the church	Acts 2:47

    b. Names used for members of the church in the New Testament:

◆ Christians	Acts 11:26; 1 Peter4:16
◆ disciples	Acts 11:29
◆ brethren	Acts 11:29)
◆ sons of God	Romans 8:14
◆ saints	Romans 1:7
◆ children of God	Romans 8:16; 1 John 3:1

2. We must restore the ordinances of the church:
   a. Baptism (Chapter 8 & Appendix)
   b. The Lord's Supper (Chapter 9)
   c. The Lord's Day (Chapter 10)
3. We must restore the financial support by tithes and offerings. (Chapter 11)
4. We must restore the government and offices of the church. (Chapter 12)
5. We must restore the mission of the church. (Chapter 13)
6. We must restore the ministries of the church. (Chapter 14)
7. We must restore worship as it was taught and practiced in the New Testament. (Chapter 15)

Chapter 8 – BAPTISM AS PRACTICED IN THE NEW TESTAMENT

There is much discussion about the origin of baptism. The first we read about baptism in the Bible is in the ministry of John the Baptizer. The Pharisees were surprised to find John baptizing people (John 1:24, 25). That suggests that it was either something new to them, or something that was not commonly seen. The baptism of John came from God (Matthew 21:25; John 1:6). God is also the source of the baptism given to the church on the day of Pentecost (Acts 2:4, 38).

WHAT WAS JOHN'S BAPTISM?
1. It was immersion of a person in water.
   - It required a lot of water (John 3:23). John often preached in places near much water (Matthew 3:5, 6).
   - Both John and the person being baptized needed to go down into the water and come up out of the water (Matthew 3:16; Mark 1:10).
2. It was a baptism of repentance in preparation for the coming of Jesus (Acts 19:4; Luke 3:8).

3. It required people to change the way they lived (Luke 3:10-14).

WHAT IS BAPTISM AS PRACTICED BY THE CHURCH?

1. It is immersion in water.
   - It requires water (Acts 8:36; 10:47).
   - Both people must go into the water and come up out of the water (Acts 8:38, 39).
2. It is for people old enough to be taught and to believe on Jesus as the Christ (Mark 16:16; Matthew 28:19; Acts 16:31-33).
3. It requires the person to recognize his sins and to repent of those sins (Acts 2:38; 22:16).
4. It is the means of receiving the Holy Spirit (Acts 2:38; 19:2-7).
5. It is a symbol of the death, burial, and resurrection of Jesus and the death of the old man of sin and the resurrection of the new man in Christ (Romans 6:2-10; Colossians 2:12).
6. It is a symbol of the ark of Noah in that it carries people to salvation (1 Peter 3:20, 21).

IN WHAT NAME ARE PEOPLE BAPTIZED?

Some people teach that baptism should be done in the name of Jesus alone (Acts 19:5; 2:38; 10:48). Others consider baptism is only effective if the person is baptized in the name of the Father, and of the Son, and of the Holy Spirit (Matthew 28:19). There are two important considerations: (a) There is no competition or jealousy among the Father, and the Son, and the Holy Spirit. There is only unity. They have one name. Notice that Matthew 28:19 says "name" not "names." In the church of Christ we follow the instructions of Jesus as found in Matthew 28:18-20, and we baptize in the "name of the Father, and of the Son, and of the Holy Spirit, "and not "in the name of Jesus only. "To argue for a 'Jesus only" position suggests a disunity with God. (b) The second concern is that people think salvation depends on saying a formula properly. They fear getting the words in the wrong order and thereby destroying the act of baptism. This is more like ancestor worship or magic than Christianity. God is not manipulated into activity by our using the proper words or rites. He looks into the hearts of men. He has given us immersion to remind us what He has done and what He requires of us—death.

HOW MANY TIMES CAN OR SHOULD A PERSON BE BAPTIZED?

Ephesians 4:5 says there is "one baptism." That is Christian baptism. Some churches baptize three times, once each for the Father, the Son, and the Holy Spirit. Others baptize people who wish to join their local church, even if the person has been baptized (immersed) already in another church. Some people want to be baptized again each time they have fallen away.

How many times is a person born? How many times do we bury a body? It would seem reasonable that a person who has believed on Jesus, has repented of his sins, confessed Jesus before men, and been buried in water and raised up out of the water, has been born anew and had his sins forgiven and has been given the indwelling gift of the Holy Spirit. God adds to the church daily those who are being saved. Baptism should not become an initiation service whereby a person joins the church.

WHEN SHOULD A PERSON BE BAPTIZED?

In the Bible, people were baptized immediately upon their belief, repentance, and confession of faith in Jesus. Some churches have the practice of having people wait until a church official is present to do the baptizing, or until a certain set of lessons has been completed before they will baptize one who wishes to become a follower of Jesus. If there is a question about the maturity of the person, it would be well to spend some time being assured that the person understands that he must die to his old ways of sin. But long delays before baptizing a repentant sinner were not the practice of the New Testament church.

WHO CAN DO THE BAPTIZING?

The New Testament does not list qualifications, but we would understand that the person doing the baptizing would be a Christian. We are taught that things must be done properly and in good order. The act of baptism should be a reverent memory of what Jesus has done for us. If that is assured, then the church should follow other New Testament lessons in ministry in deciding who can do the baptizing.

ADDITIONAL STUDY

Go through the book of Acts and study each case of baptism to see how the above questions are answered.

Chapter 9 – THE LORD'S SUPPER: SYMBOL OF A NEW COVENANT

The Lord's Supper is sometimes wrongly called the 'Passover." There is a great difference between the Passover meal and the Lord's Supper. They represent two different covenants. The Passover is part of the old covenant celebrating freedom of Israel from slavery in Egypt. It required priests, the blood of a sacrificed lamb, and bitter vegetables to remind people of what slavery in Egypt was and what God did to free them. As members of the Jewish race and religion, Jesus and His apostles were celebrating the Passover meal when Jesus ended the meal and then introduced them to the new meal, the Lord's Supper (Matthew 26:1729; Mark 14:12-25; Luke 22:7-23; 1 Corinthians 11:17-30). Jesus assigned a different meaning and symbolism to this meal of the new covenant.

Blood is required for the forgiveness of sins (Hebrews 9:22). The animal sacrifices of the old covenant could never make the worshipers perfect (Hebrews 9:9), so it was necessary that the blood of the one-time sacrifice, our High Priest, Jesus, should forever take the place of animal sacrifices (Hebrews 9:12) and open the Holy Place for us, to bring us into the presence of God (Hebrews 9:24; 10:11-14).

Therefore, Jesus called the cup a symbol of a new covenant (Matthew 26:28; Mark 14:24; Luke 22:20; 1 Corinthians 11:25). It is His blood which forgives sins. He said of the bread, "This is my body broken for you," but of the cup He said, "This cup is the new covenant in my blood." We have a new agreement with God for salvation, and it is made true by the blood of Jesus Christ.

WHO SHOULD PARTAKE OF THE LORD'S SUPPER?

In the church of Christ we usually do not forbid anyone to partake because the invitation is given by Jesus. It is the Lord's Supper. However, since it is a celebration of the new covenant, it would be reasonable to consider that it is intended for people who through the new birth of baptism are now enjoying the benefits of the new covenant. Can we partake if we have sinned? All of us are sinners (Romans 3:23). We do not partake because we are perfect, but because we have been made perfect through the blood of Jesus. We celebrate what His death has done for us.

HOW SHOULD WE PARTAKE?

There are no instructions on the order of the service, but there are warnings against disorder in the service (1 Corinthians 11:17-22), and against disorder in the life and manner of the individual (1 Corinthians 11:27-30). Too much time is wasted in useless discussions about the proper order for prayers, songs, and passing of the symbols. Jesus did not mean to make it a complicated thing, but to show us the beauty and simplicity of God's love for us.

Concern is also expressed about who should preside over the table. Again, the Bible is silent on the matter, and it is something which must be decided in light of other Bible teachings on the conduct of activities within the church. The power of the Lord's Supper is not in the person who is speaking or praying; it is not in the company that sells the bread or the cup. The power is in the saving death of Jesus and in the new covenant purchased with His blood.

WHEN SHOULD THE LORD'S SUPPER BE SERVED?

It was given by Jesus on a Thursday night (Friday by Jewish time) and observed by the church for the first time on a Sunday, the day of Pentecost. The Bible suggests that it was observed by the early church every Sunday (Acts 20:7), as were offerings (1 Corinthians 16:2). In the early church they met daily and broke bread from house to house (Acts 2:46). In the church of Christ it is our understanding that Jesus intended for the Lord's Supper to be observed each week, on the first day of the week, as part of the regular worship service. We celebrate the new covenant of salvation.

ADDITIONAL STUDY

What is the message of the Lord's Supper?
1. Jesus died for the forgiveness of sins (Matthew 26:28).
2. Jesus died for many people (Mark 14:24).
3. We eat and drink in remembrance of His death (Luke 2:19).
4. The cup and the loaf are a participation (sharing) in the death of Jesus (1 Corinthians 10:16).
5. The many small pieces of bread that come from one loaf show us that although we are many, we are one, because all Christians come from Jesus (1 Corinthians 10:17).
6. If we participate in the worship of false gods, we cannot partake of the Lord's Supper (1 Corinthians 10:21).
7. The Lord's Supper can be harmful to the partaker (1 Corinthians 11:17, 27, 30).
8. The Lord's Supper preaches (proclaims) the death of Jesus (1 Corinthians 11:26)
9. The Lord's Supper is to be observed until the return of Jesus (1 Corinthians 11:26).

Chapter 10 – THE LORD'S DAY: CELEBRATING FREEDOM

"On the Lord's Day I was in the Spirit . . ." (Revelation 1:10). This is how the apostle John described himself in worship as he was on the island of Patmos. It is the only time in the Bible that the day is called "the Lord's Day." The early church commonly used the designation "the Lord's Day" to mean the first day of the week.

ON WHAT DAY DID THE EARLY CHURCH MEET FOR WORSHIP?

The first day of the week was the time for assembled worship for the early church (1 Corinthians 16:2; Acts 20:7). It was a regular time for observing the Lord's Supper, for hearing sermons and discussions, and for making offerings to the church. It was a time for the church to come together as a family to celebrate.

Every Christian has the responsibility to worship on a daily basis. He is to pray (Luke 18:1; Ephesians 6:18), study the Bible (Acts 17:11), live a sacrificial life (Romans 12:1), and work for God (1 Corinthians 15:58). This is an individual and daily responsibility. The time for assembled worship of the church is the first day of the week.

WHY DID THE EARLY CHURCH CELEBRATE IN WORSHIP ON THE FIRST DAY OF THE WEEK?

All of the ordinances of the church find their origin in the death, burial, and resurrection of Jesus Christ. We are commanded to baptize so that the death, burial, and resurrection will be remembered (Romans 6:3-5; Colossians 2:12). We observe the Lord's Supper to remember His death (1 Corinthians 11:25, 26; Luke 22:19). In like manner, the early church met on the first day of the week to remember the day of the resurrection of Jesus (Matthew 28:1-7; Mark 16:2-7; Luke 24:1-8; John 20:1, 2), and to celebrate the day the Holy Spirit came upon them and the church was established (Acts 2:1). Pentecost was 50 days after the Passover, and the last Passover of Jesus was a "high Passover" because it was on a special Sabbath day. Jesus was crucified on Preparation Day, which was on Friday (Matthew 27:62; Luke 23:54). The following day was the Sabbath (Mark 15:42), and it was the special Sabbath (John 19:31-34). Fifty days (Pentecost) following that Sabbath day was the day the church began, and it was the first day of the week.

WHY DO WE NOT OBSERVE THE SABBATH DAY AS A DAY FOR GATHERING IN WORSHIP?

The purpose of the Sabbath was to remember the creative power of God (Genesis 2:2, 3; Exodus 16:23; 20:8-11). It was a day which was holy and it was to be remembered by resting, doing no work (Matthew 12:1-13). It was not observed by the Jews as a day for coming together to worship until the time of the exile in Babylon when synagogue worship was started. There is no Old Testament reference for gathering together to worship on the Sabbath Day.

We are urged not to allow people to judge us because we do not observe the Sabbath (Colossians 2:16, 17, 20; Galatians 4:10, 11). Christians are not under Old Testament law (Acts 15:10, 11;

Romans 4:13-25; Galatians 3:25; Colossians 2:20-23; Hebrews 9:9, 10). We live under God's grace. We are people of "the promise" (Galatians 3:19-22).

WHY DID JESUS, PAUL, AND OTHERS ATTEND SYNAGOGUES ON THE SABBATH?

It was the purpose of Jesus to be the only person to keep the law perfectly. In order to do so He needed to observe the Sabbath requirements, as well as other Old Testament laws. Those laws would not cease until He died and the church was established. Paul attended services on the Sabbath in the synagogue with the Jews because he enjoyed discussing God's Word, and because he could preach to Jews about the new freedom given by Jesus. He made many Jews angry with his preaching, and if they refused to hear about Jesus, Paul would leave the synagogue (Acts 18:7; 19:9).

As free people we are not forbidden to worship on any day of the week, or at any time of the day, but the New Testament shows the church met for worship on the first day of the week.

WHAT IS WRONG WITH TRYING TO KEEP THE OLD TESTAMENT LAW?

1. If you keep one Old Testament law, then you must keep all of the law (Galatians 3:10).
2. The law was meant to lead people to Jesus Christ, but not to be a substitute for Jesus Christ (Galatians 3:19, 24; Romans 5:20, 21).
3. Jesus fulfilled the law and instituted a new covenant (Ephesians 2:14, 15; Colossians 2:13, 14; Hebrews 7:18, 19; 8:13; 10:9).

4. The apostles instructed the church not to follow Old Testament laws:
    a. All foods are clean (Mark 7:1 8, 19; 1 Corinthians 10:25, 26; Colossians 2:1 6; 1 Timothy 4:4).
    b. Circumcision is not necessary (1 Corinthians 7:18, 19; Galatians 5:2; 6:15).
    c. Special days are no longer kept (Colossians 2:16, 17).
    d. Animal sacrifices have no value (Hebrews 9:9, 10, 12; 10:3-9)
    e. The law puts us back into slavery. We have freedom in Jesus Christ (Galatians 5:1).

SUMMARY

We observe the first day of the week, the Lord's Day, as a time for gathering the church together for worship. At that time we observe the Lord's Supper, make offerings, and give sermons and lessons. It is a time of praise as we remember the death, burial, and resurrection of Jesus, as well as the coming of the Holy Spirit to the church.

The Sabbath was a day of rest to remember the creative work of God. It was not originally a day for gathering of people together for worship, although it later became such a day. To make the Sabbath Day binding because it is part of the law would require making all of the law binding on Christians, and this was forbidden by the apostles. Jesus died to free us from sin and from the law.

ADDITIONAL STUDY

1. Discuss Hebrews 4:1-11. The Christian sabbath is our rest in heaven.

2. Discuss worship as a condition of the heart, rather than as ceremonial acts. (Psalm 51:3-6; 1 Samuel 15:19-23; Micah 6:6-8; Isaiah 1:10-17; Malachi 1:10-14; Matthew 7:21)

3. Discuss why the new day, the Lord's Day, is a celebration of the new covenant. (Jeremiah 31:31-34; Hebrews 8:7-13.)

Chapter 11 – TITHES AND OFFERINGS

"And all the tithe of the land, whether of the seed of the land, or of the fruit of the tree, is the Lord's; it is holy unto the Lord." (Leviticus 27:30; KJV).

Under the Old Testament law, God commanded that tithes and offerings be given to Him. The verse above from Leviticus tells us that the tithe belonged to the Lord as a holy gift. There were rewards for those who followed God's commands and punishments for those who disobeyed Him.

WHAT IS A TITHE?

A tithe is one tenth portion. People often think of tithes in terms of money, but from the verse above we see that God's portion was to be given from everything that people received. If ten goats or chickens were born in a year, one of each ten was God's. If the field or the garden produced ten bags or ten baskets of fruit, then one of each ten was God's. Whether it was cattle, fowls, eggs, corn or pots, one of each ten was to be given to God as a holy tithe.

WHEN DID THE PRACTICE OF TITHING BEGIN?

It is a very old practice that began before history was written down, and before Moses gave the law to the children of Israel. The first we read of it is in Genesis 14:18-20 when Abraham gave a tithe of all he got from the battle with the kings. This tithe was given to the priest Melchizedek. In Hebrews 7:1-10, the gift of the tithe to Melchizedek is shown to represent a continuing practice of honoring the Son of God (Hebrews 7:3, 8). We do not know when the practice began, but we do know that God ordained it as a way to show honor and respect to one who is spiritually greater than we are.

WARNINGS TO THOSE WHO FAIL TO GIVE

The prophet Malachi warned people about robbing God (Malachi 3:8-12). His concern was that they were keeping the best portion for themselves and were bringing sick and injured animals to God as sacrificial gifts (Malachi 1:13, 14). King Saul disobeyed God's command and kept things for his own use and he lost his kingdom (1 Samuel 15:7-11). Achan (Joshua 7:24-26) and Ananias and Sapphira (Acts 5:1-11) kept offerings that belonged to God and they died for their sin. Robbing God has its punishment.

WHAT DOES THE NEW TESTAMENT TEACH ABOUT GIVING OF OFFERINGS?

1. It teaches that Jesus is worthy of being given the tithe (Hebrews 7:1-10).
2. It teaches us that God is the perfect example of giving.
   a. Romans 5:8 – God gave His Son while we were still sinners.
   b. James 1:5 – God gives generously.
   c. James 1:17 – God's gifts are perfect.

d. *2* Corinthians 9:15 – God's gift is beyond describing.

e. *2* Corinthians 8:9 – Jesus became poor for us. He gave until He was poor.

3. It teaches that God loves those who give themselves before they give the offering (2 Corinthians 8:5).

4. Our giving is to be proportional to what we have received (1 Corinthians 16:2).

5. Our reward from God is proportional to our giving (Luke 6:38; 2 Corinthians 9:6, 10, 11).

6. Christian giving puts members of the church on an equality (2 Corinthians 8:13, 14).

7. Christian giving is a test of our love (2 Corinthians 8:8, 24).

8. Giving helps us to experience the grace of God (2 Corinthians 8:1).

9. Each Christian must decide how much he will give (2 Corinthians 8:3, 4).

10. Our giving is an expression of our thanks to God (2 Corinthians 9:12).

11. Giving should be done regularly, weekly (1 Corinthians 16:2).

12. Giving must be done willingly and cheerfully (2 Corinthians 9:7).

13. Our giving must be done quietly so as not to impress others (Matthew 6:1-4).

ADDITIONAL STUDY

Jesus taught much about the use of our personal possessions. In addition to parts from the Sermon on the Mountain (Matthew chapters 5-7), Jesus gave many other lessons. Examine the following which are found in the Gospel of Luke:

1. There are things in life more important than wealth (Luke 4:4).
2. There are things more important even than the tithe (Luke 11:42).
3. Greed keeps people from giving to God (Luke 12:29-31; 16:13).
4. Fear of poverty keeps people from giving to God (Luke 12:3234).
5. Personal wealth may keep us out of Heaven (Luke 18:18-25; 21:1-4).

Giving is one of the weak areas of practice among members of the churches of Christ, and it keeps us from enjoying the grace and the power of God.

Chapter 12 – THE GOVERNMENT OF THE CHURCH

Christ's church is a living institution with Jesus himself the founder, the head, and the cornerstone (Colossians 1:18; Ephesians 2:19, 20). At first there were apostles and other members of the church (Acts 2), but as the numbers grew and problems arose, it was seen that there needed to be some others who would care for the day-to-day needs of the church. In Acts chapter 6 we read about seven men being chosen to look after these needs. The Bible describes them as "willing servants" which is the meaning of the word "deacon." Sometimes they are referred to as the first deacons, although this title is not used in the passage. Two of them were known to be very good preachers, Stephen and Philip. Philip is later called an evangelist.

On their return journey from their first missionary work, Paul and Barnabas appointed elders in all the churches where they had preached (Acts 14:23). These elders were to look after the churches.

In the New Testament there are a number of offices mentioned, but it is likely that three of them were to be permanent offices: elders, deacons, and evangelists (ministers, preachers). This lesson will consider only these three offices in the church.

ELDERS, BISHOPS, OVERSEERS

These three words (elders, bishops, overseers) are used interchangeably to refer to the same office in the church (1 Peter 5:1; 1 Timothy 3:1; 1 Timothy 5:1; Ephesians 4:11; Philippians 1:1). However, the word used is almost always in the plural form. We do not see any example in Scripture where one elder (bishop) ruled over a number of churches. There were a number of elders who worked together to guide the local church, or at least a church in a local area like Ephesus or Antioch (Acts 20:17-37).

How does a church determine who should have the office of elder? The Bible gives us lists of qualities that are to be found in such men (1 Timothy 3:1-7; Titus 1:5-9). We will not discuss these required qualities, but rather the work of the elder.

1. Elders are to govern the church (1 Timothy 3:5; 5:17), but by good example rather than by force (1 Peter 5:3).
2. They are to look after the spiritual needs of the church (1 Peter 5:2).
3. They are to equip the church to build it up (Ephesians 4:12).
4. They must protect the church from false teachers (Acts 20:28-30) by holding to the truth and refuting false doctrine (Titus 1:9).
5. They are to visit the sick and pray for them (James 5:14).
6. They are to do all these things by having an aptitude for teaching (1 Timothy 3:2).

DEACONS

The character and the life of the deacon is very much like that of the elder (1 Timothy 3:8-12) except that he need not have been a Christian as long as the elder (1 Timothy 3:6). There is not much said about the work of deacons. The word "deacon" means a 'Willing servant." If those men chosen to help the apostles in Acts chapter 6 were meant to be examples of the work of the deacons, then we see them serving so as to give their leaders more time "for prayer and the ministry of the word." They would take responsibility for much of the daily activities needed to care for the physical needs of the church.

THE EVANGELIST (PREACHER, MINISTER)

There are numbers of names which designate the work of those who spend their time in the preaching of the Word. There was an office (Acts 21:8), a specific work (2 Timothy 4:5), for those who were called to preach the gospel. Paul refers to this work as that of a minister (1 Timothy 4:6). Some examples of men who were called to this office were Timothy, Titus, Philip, John Mark, and Tychicus (Acts 21:8; 2 Timothy 4:5; 1 Thessalonians 3:2; Ephesians 6:21; Acts 13:5). Timothy and Silvanus are also called preachers.

Men who devote themselves to the preaching of the gospel should get their living from the gospel (1 Corinthians 9:7-13). Those who receive the instruction should share all good things with their instructor (Galatians 6:6).

Such men are to be respected for their hard work (1 Thessalonians 5:12, 13), but the respect given is not that which belongs to God. Titles such as "Father' or "Reverend" are reserved to be used for God alone (Matthew 23:9; Psalm 111:9).

ADDITIONAL STUDY

In 1 Timothy 4:6-16, Paul lists qualities which should be found in an excellent minister of the gospel. Study the passage to see how many you can find.

1. He warns people of error – verse 6 (Hebrews 13:17).
2. He is a student of the Bible – verse 6 (1 Peter 2:2; 2 Timothy 2:15; Ephesians 6:17; Colossians 3:16; 2 Timothy 3:16, 17).

3. He avoids useless discussion – verse 7 (1 Timothy 1:4).

4. He is a godly person – verse 7 (1 Corinthians 9:27; 2 Timothy 2:3-5).

5. He is a hard-working person – verse 10 (1 Corinthians 3:11 - 15).

6. He teaches with authority – verse 11 (Titus 2:15).

7. He is an example for others to follow – verse 12 (1 Corinthians 4:16; 1 Corinthians 10:31-33; Philippians 3:17; 4:9; 1 Thessalonians 1:5, 6; 2 Thessalonians 3:7, 9).

Chapter 13 – THE MISSION OF THE CHURCH

The reason Jesus came to earth was that He might provide away for people to be free from the slavery and the punishment of sin. That is what we celebrate each first day of the week when we partake of the Lord's Supper (Luke 19:10; John 14:6). However, since the forgiveness of sin required the death of Jesus, His resurrection, and His return to Heaven, it was necessary that He entrust the completion of His ministry to others.

Before Jesus returned to Heaven, He commissioned His disciples to go to all the nations of the world to make disciples, to baptize them, and to teach them everything that He had taught (Matthew 28:18-20; Mark 16:15, 16; Luke 24:46-49; John 20:21). So that His followers could accomplish this mission, Jesus promised to give them the Holy Spirit as a helper, guiding them in the truth and giving them power (Acts 1:8; John 16:13-15).

GOD'S ETERNAL PURPOSE

Following the sin of Adam and Eve, God promised that He would bring defeat to Satan (Genesis 3:15). He chose Abraham to be the father of a great nation through whom all the people of the earth would be blessed (Genesis 12:3). It was God's eternal plan that Jesus come to earth and that redemption come through His blood (Ephesians 1:7-10). It was also God's eternal plan that the church would reveal the purpose He accomplished in Jesus Christ (Ephesians 3:10-12). So the mission of the church is to make God's plan for salvation known to all the peoples of the earth.

THE THREE-FOLD MISSION OF THE CHURCH

In Matthew 28:18-20, Jesus told His disciples to do three things:

1. *They were to make disciples from all the nations.*

   A disciple is a learner. He is one who studies his master so that he may become like his master. We are to make disciples, leading people to learn to be like Jesus. We teach not only His history but His person.

   People from all nations are to become disciples of Jesus. In order for this to happen, it is necessary for Christians to have a passion for the lost and a vision that encompasses the whole earth. Each congregation must understand that it has a responsibility to be as involved in missionary work as was the church at Antioch. See Acts 13:1-3. A careful reading of this text will reveal that at Antioch the emphasis is upon the church and sending, not on the missionary and going. This emphasis needs to be maintained today.

2. *They are to baptize those disciples in the name of the Father, and of the Son, and of the Holy Spirit.*

   This is covered in chapter 8, but it is worth repeating that the disciple comes into a saving relationship with Jesus through baptism.

3. *They are to teach the baptized disciples to follow all of the teachings of Jesus.*

   This is a very important part of our mission. Many Christians are ignorant of the teachings of Jesus. It is the duty of the leaders of the church to plan ways to instruct new members and to improve the knowledge of the older members about all that Jesus taught. Only then will the church be strong.

ADDITIONAL STUDY

1. See how Jesus talked to people who needed salvation:
   - Nicodemus   John 3:1-21
   - The Samaritan woman   John 4:1-38
   - The woman caught in adultery   John 8:1-11
   - The man born blind   John 9:1-38

2. The Holy Spirit often does the work before we do. Acts 2:38; 8:26-40; 9:1-17; 10:1-48

3. Because you may not always have your Bible with you, here are some verses that are good to memorize:
   - Romans 3:23 – All have sinned
   - Romans 6:23 – God has provided an answer to sin
   - Acts 4:12 – Salvation is found only in Jesus
   - Luke 13:1-5 – People must repent
   - Matthew 10:32, 33 – People must confess Jesus before men
   - Acts 2:38 – Forgiveness of sin and the gift of the Holy Spirit come by baptism
   - 1 John 5:11-13 – Eternal life is an assured promise

Chapter 14 – THE MINISTRIES OF THE CHURCH

God cares for the many needs of people. One of the tasks of angels is to care for such needs (Psalm 91:11; Hebrews 1:14). Through the church the human and spiritual needs of people are also satisfied. To make our service more effective, God has given special spiritual ministries to people within the church. Some of these spiritual gifts are discussed by Paul in his letter to the church in Rome. The gifts listed are (1) preaching, (2) serving others, (3) teaching, (4) encouraging, (5) contributing to the needs of others, and (6) leadership (Romans 12:6-8). We shall briefly discuss these ministries of the church.

THE MINISTRY OF PREACHING

How can they hear without someone preaching to them?" (Romans 10:14). The salvation of the world depends on the ministry of preaching. Paul said, "For Christ did not send me to baptize, but to preach the gospel" (1 Corinthians 1:17). He also said, "God was pleased through the foolishness of what was preached to save those who believe" (1 Corinthians 1:21). Paul told Timothy to always be prepared to preach, and to preach (2 Timothy 4:2). Jesus chose preaching as one of His most important ways to reveal God to men.

The ministry of good Bible preaching is one of the most important ministries of the church, and some have been gifted for this ministry.

THE MINISTRY OF SERVING OTHERS

One of the first problems to arise in the church was what to do about the needs of widows (Acts 6:1), and seven men who were trusted were chosen to see that this ministry was done well. There are a number of ministries of serving:

1. Serving widows and orphans – James 1:27
2. Caring for the sick – James 5:14, 15
3. Providing hospitality – Romans 12:13. Providing hospitality is a quality of an elder (1 Timothy 3:2; Titus 1:8), and it is an admonition to Christians (Hebrews 13:2; 1 Peter 4:9).

THE MINISTRY OF TEACHING

1. Elders of the church are to be able to teach (1 Timothy 3:2).
2. Christians should teach one another (Colossians 3:16; 2 Timothy 2:24).
3. Older women are to teach younger women (Titus 2:3-5).

THE MINISTRY OF ENCOURAGING

Barnabas was admired by the early church because he was an encourager (Acts 4:36). He encouraged Paul when others were afraid of him (Acts 11:25, 26). When the dispute arose over John Mark, it was Barnabas who helped John Mark to continue preaching (Acts 15:37-40). Christians are told to encourage one another. It helps us to overcome fear (Matthew 10:31).

THE MINISTRY OF CONTRIBUTING TO THE NEEDS OF OTHERS

God has a deep concern for the poor (Proverbs 19:17; Ezekiel 16:49). Contributing to the needs of the poor was taught by Jesus (Luke 12:33) and required by the apostles (Galatians 2:10). The early church learned how to give by giving to the needs of the poor, first by making common use of their property in Jerusalem (Acts 2:45), and later by gathering money to send to those suffering from famine in Jerusalem (1 Corinthians 16:2; 2 Corinthians 9:1-5). God has gifted some people with the ability to have more possessions than others. These must use their possessions to help the poor. Such ministry must be done in the name of Jesus and to His honor and not for personal glory.

THE MINISTRY OF LEADERSHIP

There are not many people who can lead others well. Some leaders like the power they have over others and use it for their own gain. The gift of leadership is an important one for the church, but we must remember that a good leader leads by example (1 Peter 5:1-4).

ADDITIONAL STUDY

1. The importance in ministry is not what ministry we have, but in how we use it (Matthew 25:14-30; Romans 12:6; 1 Corinthians 4:7).

2. Jesus used parables to teach about how we should use our ministry.
   - The Good Samaritan   Luke 10:25-37
   - The Rich Man and Lazarus   Luke 16:19-31
   - The Talents   Matthew 25:14-30
   - The Sheep and the Goats   Matthew 25:31-46

3. AIDS

In these days when the world is plagued with AIDS, the church must be at the front in showing love to the victims and the families of those with AIDS. Some people fear ministry to AIDS sufferers because they feel that it is a judgment from God and we should not interfere with God's punishment of sinners. Others are afraid that if they touch people with AIDS, they will get the disease themselves.

While it is true that all sin reaps its own harvest, this should not cause us to be arrogant toward the lost and unwilling to minister to them. While caution should be exercised in dealing with all diseases, an unreasonable fear of AIDS must not allow us to fail to witness to people for whom Christ died.

Chapter 15 – PUBLIC AND PRIVATE WORSHIP

"Worship" means to show respect, to bow down, to give reverence and honor, to love and adore. God does not permit worship to be given to any gods, idols, or to people (Exodus 20:1-6). He forbids the worship of ancestors or other spirits (Deuteronomy 18:10-13; Leviticus 19:31; Revelation 21:8). His faithful followers never bowed down to false gods (Daniel 3:1-30), neither would they accept worship from other men (Acts 14:11-18). Worship is for God alone.

King David was deeply loved by God because David was a man who worshiped God with all of his heart (1 Kings 14:8; 15:5). David failed God in many ways with terrible sin, but he returned to God in worship and God loved him.

PUBLIC WORSHIP

We are instructed to gather ourselves together for worship (Hebrews 10:25). When the church gathers together, it is not for outward forms of worship, which are called "ritual." God has always condemned mere outward forms of worship (Isaiah 1:1017; Malachi 1:10-14). Worship is a condition of the heart (John 4:23, 24; Luke 18:9-14).

There are four elements in public worship which are mentioned in Acts 2:42, and these constitute the basis for our public worship. They are:

1. *Continuing steadfastly in the apostles' doctrine* (Romans 16:17; 1 Corinthians 1:21; Galatians 1:6-9; 1 Timothy 4:16; 2 John 9, 10). This includes the public preaching, teaching, and discussion of the Word of God.

2. *The breaking of bread* (the Lord's Supper) (Chapter 8).

3. *Prayer* (Acts 4:31; 12:5-11; Philippians 4:6; Hebrews 4:16; James 4:3).

4. *Fellowship of sharing* (2 Corinthians 8:4; Galatians 6:6; Hebrews 13:16) which includes sharing of ourselves with each other, as well as sharing our possessions (Acts 2:44, 45).

Paul reminded the church that their worship should be orderly (1 Corinthians 14:40), and that wrong worship causes spiritual sickness (1 Corinthians 11:30). Public worship is not a matter of getting four things done on a Sunday morning; it is honoring God and celebrating His love for us.

PRIVATE WORSHIP

Private worship was taught by Jesus (Matthew 6:5, 6). Many people who attend public worship services regularly do not have any private time spent in worship. Jesus found much strength in His time alone with God (Luke 4:42). He often spent the whole night praying (Luke 6:12).

When Jesus spoke to Nicodemus (John 3:1-21), He said that it is necessary to be born of the water and of the Spirit. A believer does that by being immersed in water in baptism, and by having the Holy Spirit give birth to spirit in the life of the believer (John 3:6). When the Spirit gives birth to a new spirit within us, it will be demonstrated by the fruit that it produces (Galatians 5:22-24). That fruit grows and develops with time spent in private worship. We are told to be imitators of Jesus (Ephesians 5:1-4). When we imitate Jesus, we will develop into new people. Bad language will give way to thanksgiving; complaining will give way to praise and to prayer.

In the Psalms, we see good examples of private worship. In private worship:

1. We meditate (Psalm 1:2; 39:3; 63:6; 145:5). We are taught that our minds control our behavior (Matthew 15:18; Luke 6:45), so our thinking is very important to what kind of person we are.
2. We read the Bible (Psalm 119:105, 111, 112). It is God speaking to us (2 Timothy 3:14-17).
3. We pray. Most of the Psalms are prayers which were meant for singing.

Other Scriptures on prayer include Acts 10:9; Ephesians 6:18; 1 Thessalonians 5:17; James 5:13.

ADDITIONAL STUDY

Worship is a condition of the heart. Its most sincere quality is prayer. Great people of the Bible were people of earnest and sincere prayer. The following are examples of their successful prayer life:

◆ Abraham	Genesis 18:23-33
◆ Jacob	Genesis 32:24-30
◆ Moses	Deuteronomy 9:18-21
◆ Jesus	Luke 22:41-46
◆ Early Christians	Acts 12:5-17
◆ Elijah	James 5:17, 18

Chapter 16 – ETERNITY

Jesus is coming again! He promised His followers that He would come back for them (John 14:3). When Jesus was taken into Heaven, two angels appeared and told His disciples that they would see Him return again (Acts 1:11). The book of Revelation says, "Every eye will see him, even those who pierced him" (Revelation 1:7). In many of His parables, Jesus taught about His return and the judgment to come:

- The Net   Matthew 13:47-50
- Workers in the Vineyard   Matthew 20:1-16
- Weeds in the Field   Matthew 13:24-30
- The Wedding Feast   Matthew 22:1-14
- The Ten Virgins   Matthew 25:1-13
- The Talents   Matthew 25:14-30
- The Sheep and Goats   Matthew 25:31-46
- Rich Man and Lazarus   Luke 16:19-31

In each of these parables there is a reward for the faithful and punishment for those who are found unfaithful. Jesus clearly taught that there is a Heaven and a Hell.

HELL

Hell is a place prepared for Satan and his angels (Matthew 25:41). Evil people will be there also (1 Corinthians 6:9, 10; Romans 2:8; Revelation 21:8; 22:15). Those who do not believe in Jesus will be judged and punished for their sins (John 3:18, 36).

What is Hell like? It is called a place of fire and darkness (Matthew 5:22; 22:13). Since God is not there no good will be found in Hell and the punishment will be everlasting (2 Thessalonians 1:9).

There are several words in the Bible which are translated "Hell." Sheol is a Hebrew word which means a pit or a grave, or the place of the dead. The similar Greek word is hades, a place where the dead wait. The Bible also uses the word "Gehenna," a name given to the place near Jerusalem where all the stinking rubbish from the city was collected and burned. It was a rotten place full of worms and sickening smells. It is this word which is chosen most correctly to picture Hell.

HEAVEN

Because of Christ, we can escape the punishment of Hell. Jesus has prepared Heaven for His followers (John 14:2, 3; 1 Peter 1:35). In Heaven we will see the angels (Luke 2:13) and Jesus seated at the right hand of the Father (Colossians 3:1; Hebrews 9:24; 12:22-24). We will be new creatures who will have new bodies (1 Corinthians 15:40-49) so that we can be like Jesus (Philippians 3:21).

The apostle John found human words impossible to describe the beauty of Heaven or the ugliness of Hell (book of Revelation). It is frightening to know that there is no way to pass from Hell to Heaven (Luke 16:26), but both places must be entered from earth (Luke 16:22, 23). We must be prepared.

WHEN AND HOW WILL JESUS RETURN?

People are interested in knowing the time when Jesus will return. The apostles asked to know the time (Matthew 24:3), but Jesus said it was a time which was known only by God, so people must always be prepared (Matthew 24:36-51). Jesus said that He will come when it is least expected (Luke 12:40). He comes as a thief (Revelation 16:15) so we must always be ready (1 Thessalonians 5:2; Philippians 4:5; Hebrews 10:37; James 5:8; Revelation 3:11; 22:7, 20).

Some people try to teach that they know the exact plans and events of the return of Jesus. They use Revelation 20:1-10, Matthew 24, Daniel 7, 11 and 12 to prove their ideas. There are many theories and those teaching them do not agree. When asked about the time, Jesus said, Be ready "

ADDITIONAL STUDY

1. The New Testament teaches us that we have certain obligations and tasks because of the unexpected return of Jesus.
   a. We must regularly observe the Lord's Supper (1 Corinthians 11:26).
   b. We must live pure lives loving one another (1 Thessalonians 3:11-13; 5:23; Titus 2:11-13; 1 John 3:2, 3).
   c. We must watch and be faithful (Mark 13:33-37; 1 John 2:28).
   d. We should not judge (1 Corinthians 4:3-5).
   e. We must be busy preaching (2 Timothy 4:1, 2).
   f. We must care for the church (1 Peter 5:2-4).
   g. We must have zeal for the lost (1 Thessalonians 1:9, 10; 2:19, 20).

2. What things will happen when Jesus returns?
   a. The dead will rise at His return (1 Corinthians 15:23).
   b. Our present bodies will change (1 Corinthians 15:51, 52; 1 John 3:1, 2).
   c. Jesus will reward the faithful (2 Timothy 4:7, 8; 1 Peter 5:4).
   d. Forgiveness of sins and salvation are associated with the return of Jesus (Hebrews 9:14-28).

Appendix – BAPTISM - Written by Dr. Lewis A. Foster

I. THE IMPORTANCE OF BAPTISM

In the life of Christ. Jesus came to the Jordan to be baptized by John the Baptist to fulfill all righteousness. This marks the beginning of His public ministry. The importance of this event is seen as the voice of God acknowledges His Son, the Holy Spirit descends upon Him, and all the Gospel writers describe the scene (Matthew 3:1317; Mark 1:9-1 1; Luke 3:21, 22; John 1:29-34).

In the commands of Christ. The last words of a loved one are always held in highest importance. When Jesus left this earth, He delivered to the disciples the Great Commission. Despite the extreme brevity of the instruction, combined with an explicit statement of His full authority, Jesus commanded baptism (Matthew 28:19, 20; Mark 16:15, 16).

In the record of conversions. The Book of Acts tells of the founding and spread of the early church. One should note that each of the conversions explicitly described includes baptism (Acts 2:38, 41 – Pentecost; 8:32-38 – Philip and the eunuch; 9:18, 22:12-16 - Saul; 10:45-48 – Cornelius; 16:14, 15 – Lydia; 16:33, 34 – Philippian jailor).

In the summary of apostolic teaching. It is to be remembered that the epistles are written to persons already Christians. Despite this fact the subject of baptism arises frequently because of its importance in the teaching of the apostles; for example, "One Lord, one faith, one baptism" (Ephesians 4: 5); "For by one Spirit are we all baptized into one body" (1 Corinthians 12:13); "The like figure whereunto even baptism doth also now save us... by the resurrection of Jesus Christ" (1 Peter 3:21).

II. THE MEANING OF BAPTISM

An act of submission – in obedience to Christ. Since man is unable to earn salvation, it is necessary that he receive God's gift on God's terms. Christ has commanded baptism of His followers, and when man complies with this expressed will of God, he indicates a submission of his own will to God ("What shall we do? Repent, and be baptized.... "- Acts 2:37, 38; "Then they that gladly received his word were baptized"-Acts 2:41).

A burial – in the likeness of Christ's death. God has not arbitrarily chosen that man submit to baptism. There is a deeper meaning in the act itself. As Christ fulfilled the will of God, the most important events in His life were the death, burial, and resurrection. In similar fashion, before a person becomes a Christian, he must die to sin and be buried in the water in a likeness of Christ's death ("Know ye not, that so many of us as were baptized into Jesus Christ were baptized into his death. Therefore we are buried with him by baptism into death. . . "- Romans 6:3, 4a. "Buried with him in baptism... "Colossians 2:12).

A washing – for the remission of sins. The association of water and cleansing is universal. It is entirely appropriate that God should have chosen an act which includes water as significant to the cleansing of our souls. Although no magical quality is attributed to the water itself, God has associated the forgiveness of sins with the blood of Christ and the waters of baptism ("Repent, and be baptized... for the remission of sins." - Acts 2:38; Arise, and be baptized, and wash away thy sins."— Acts 22:16).

A union – with the person of Christ. Although baptism is not the only requirement in becoming a Christian, it appears at the threshold marking the entrance. At baptism, one puts on Jesus Christ ("For as many of you as have been baptized into Christ have put on Christ."— Galatians 3:27); in turn he is added to the body of Christ. ("Then they that gladly received his word were baptized: and the same day there were added unto them about three thousand souls." - Acts 2:41; "For by one Spirit are we all baptized into one body."— I Corinthians 12:13a).

A new birth – associated with the gift of the Spirit. Even as the life of Christ did not end with His burial but led to His final victory over sin and death, so baptism for the Christian becomes the moment of new birth, a raising to the newness of life and the reception of the gift of the Holy Spirit ("that like as Christ was raised up from the dead by the glory of the Father, even so we also should walk in newness of life." - Romans 6:4b; "Jesus answered, Verily, verily, I say unto thee, Except a man be born of water and of the Spirit, he cannot enter into the kingdom of God." - John 3:5).

III. THE ACTION OF BAPTISM

The language demands immersion. In each case that baptism is commanded the word baptidzo or one of its derivatives is used. The meaning of this Greek word is given as follows: "dip, plunge. . ." (H. B. Liddell and R. Scott, A Greek-English Lexicon, 9th edition, 1953); "dip, immerse...." (W. F. Arndt and F. W. Gingrich, A Greek-English Lexicon of the New Testament and Other Early Literature, 1957); see also J. H. Thayer, A Greek-English Lexicon of the New Testament, 1889.

The Greek language has other specific words for "sprinkle" (rantidzo) or "pour" (cheo). When the generic meaning -"wash" is used of baptidzo, it necessarily carries with it the specific meaning "by immersion" (see Campbell-Rice Debate, p. 99).

The circumstances describe immersion. It is noteworthy that all of the attending details of New Testament baptism fit immersion. Not only water, but much water was necessary ("And John also was baptizing in Aenon near to Salim, because there was much water there."—John 3:23). Not only is the presence of water made clear, but in each case, which is made explicit, they came to the water, the water was not brought to them ("and they went down both into the water, both Philip and the eunuch; and he baptized him." —Acts 8:38).

The figures picture immersion. Only immersion answers the demand made by the various figures drawn from baptism. It is a burial, a planting, a washing (buried with Christ— Romans 6:4; planted with Christ— Romans 6:5, (KJV); wash away thy sins—Acts 22:16; completely encompassed by sea and cloud— I Corinthians 10:2).

History sustains immersion. Although other practices have been introduced as substitutes, history sustains that these are changes from the original practice of immersion. The earliest historical example of pouring occurred in about A. D. 250. This was administered because of Novation's illness and was later called in question (Eusebius, Hist. ecel. 6, 43, 14, 15). Earlier references to practices other than immersion either give preference to immersion or do not deny the originality of immersion (The Didache, written in the second century, maintained that pouring was acceptable, but only in cases where sufficient water for immersion was not available, The Didache 7). The Roman Catholic Church is the earliest source of authority for a change from immersion. Clement V formally recognized sprinkling (but water must flow) as valid baptism in 1305.

IV. THOSE ELIGIBLE FOR BAPTISM

A believer. Although a person will never reach complete knowledge of Jesus Christ in this world, it is necessary that initial belief in Jesus Christ as the Son of God precede the action of baptism. Thus a person too young to believe is too young to be baptized in accordance with New Testament example. Irenaeus, A. D. 180, provides the earliest reference to possible infant baptism (Against Heresies 2, 22, 4); but this is contrary to New Testament language, "He that believeth and is baptized shall be saved. – (Mark 16:16).

A repentant believer. Intellectual assent to believe what the Scripture teaches must be accompanied with a heartfelt change of life ("Then Peter said unto them, Repent, and be baptized every one of you in the name of Jesus Christ for the remission of sins, and ye shall receive the gift of the Holy Spirit. "– Acts 2:38).